Stewards of Joy

Taking Care of
and Sharing
the Gift of Faith

Stewards of Joy

Taking Care of and Sharing the Gift of Faith

Daniel Conway

Saint Catherine of Siena Press
Indianapolis

To order additional copies of this book:
888-232-1492
www.saintcathpress.com
www.danconwayrsi.com

Printed in the United States of America.
ISBN-13: 978-0-9762284-8-6
ISBN-10: 0-9762284-8-3
Library of Congress Control Number: 2007924310

The front cover representation of the Visitation is from Holy Rosary Catholic Church in Seattle, Washington. The stained glass window depicts the joy filled encounter between the Blessed Virgin Mary and her kinswoman Elizabeth (Lk. 1:39-56). In their Pastoral Letter on Stewardship, the Bishops of the United States emphasized that it is Mary who exemplifies the perfect steward—she who proclaimed to Elizabeth the joyful words of the Magnificat, "My soul magnifies the Lord, and my spirit rejoices in God my Savior." Photography by Brock Mason, Brock Mason Photography, Seattle, WA
Cover design by Joseph Sadlier
Back cover photograph by Michael Wayne Walker, Portraits of Distinction, Plano, TX

✠

Sharon and I dedicate this book
to our parents and families
who first shared with us the joy of their Catholic faith.

May we share this precious gift of faith
gratefully, responsibly, and generously—
that in all things God may be glorified

✠

CONTENTS

PREFACE

With style and warmth, Dan Conway tells the story of his love for God and Church, for spouse and family. *Stewards of Joy* is a beguiling work. It's the story of one gifted man's generous response to Jesus' invitation to discipleship, "Love one another as I have loved you."

When Dan Conway did a study of the Archdiocese of Louisville some years ago—we were just getting into strategic planning—I asked him simplistically what we needed to get moving. "You need me," he said, "or someone like me." This was not just refreshing candor on his part, it was the absolute truth. He got us going in so many different ways. And although we've come a long way since then, the values and methods Dan brought us are still firmly in place: his hand is visible everywhere.

What ultimately drives a man like Dan Conway is his awareness of God's love for him. It is a love that quickens everything we think and do, a love that calls us to use everything given to us for God's glory. That love fills Dan Conway's life as well as his story.

Thomas C. Kelly, O.P.
Archbishop of Louisville

FOREWORD
CLAIMING OUR PARENTS' FAITH AS OUR OWN

My very first childhood memory is of my mother telling my sister and me the Christmas story. I recall vividly her descriptions of Mary, Joseph, and the Baby Jesus surrounded by shepherds and farm animals in the stable at Bethlehem. I was three years old. My sister was two. And my mother was handing on to us her faith.

My parents took their Catholic faith seriously. In their later years, they were daily communicants, but even when they were young parents raising a large family, practicing their faith was a priority. I remember going to the 6 a.m. weekday Mass with my father. The organist sang the acclamations in Latin and it's impossible to describe the mysterious sensations I felt kneeling beside my father in the semi-dark Church surrounded by those strange sounds. And when we attended the noon Mass during the week as elementary school students, I could always tell when my mother was in the back of Church because of her distinctive smoker's cough. She wore a long raincoat that covered her very unladylike Bermuda shorts, and she always arrived at the last possible minute—just as the altar boy rang the bell signaling the start of Mass.

My parents had a hard life in many ways, but they were always grateful for the gifts God gave them. When the time came to celebrate their 50th wedding anniversary, they chose to invite their immediate family members and close friends to the early morning Mass at their parish followed by brunch. They had long before recognized that their marriage was a gift from God, and they wanted to celebrate with the Church.

Their Catholic faith gave meaning to my parents' life. It was a source of hope and comfort during difficult times. It was where they found peace and encouragement. It was a gift that they cherished, and a privilege that they never took for granted.

During my teen-age years I struggled to accept my parents' faith. I was too smart, too stubborn, and too full of myself to see that the gift they had handed on to me was something really important—the key to all the questions I was asking and the way to find the freedom and happiness that I was searching for. I see now that the struggle was itself a gift. I didn't simply write-off the Catholic faith as "old fashioned." I didn't choose one of the alternate paths available to young people in the late 1960s. I argued, fought against it, and tried as hard as I could to reject the way of life my parents taught me. But like Francis Thompson's *The Hound of Heaven*, which was one of my mother's favorite poems, I was pursued by God and, in the end, I surrendered.

Years later I was comforted by the fact that St. Augustine experienced a similar struggle (obviously with greater intensity commensurate with his greater gifts and distinctive personality). Writing about Augustine's conversion, Romano Guardini says that an individual's personal struggle with the concept of God can be characterized as "the wrestling of the self-asserting individual attempting, on the one hand, to create a world on his own strength, by his own standards; on the other, the grace of God, demanding self-surrender, obedience, and the stride into faith and love."

Mine was not a dramatic conversion, but it was a genuine turning around that changed the course of my life. I credit this change of heart to the Benedictine monks of Saint Meinrad Archabbey, who helped me see my faith in a totally new light—as something that mature, gifted, intelligent men and women can commit their whole lives to. At Saint Meinrad, I discovered what it means to believe, to worship, to sacrifice and to rejoice. The monks of Saint Meinrad showed me by their words and example, by their prayer and work, by their human weakness and their striving for holiness, that the Catholic faith—my faith—is the answer to life's questions. It is what I believe in spite of my doubts and confusion. It is how I want to live in spite of my willfulness and sin. The Catholic faith is my way to Jesus. It is my way to heaven—my way to truth and love and happiness. I saw this very clearly when I was a student at Saint Meinrad in the 1970s. The faculty there taught me everything I as an adult know about the Christian life and about the teaching and practice of the Catholic Church. They helped me accept and deepen the faith that my parents gave me. I am forever grateful to Saint Meinrad—my spiritual home—for passing on to me the wisdom of the Catholic tradition and the joy of continuing conversion to Christ, the distinctive Benedictine vow.

Ultimately, the monks of Saint Meinrad helped me see that my vocation was to marry and have children. By God's grace I married Sharon, whose faith is deep and strong and unshakable. She has been an incredible companion on my life's journey. Her constant, loving care for our children has been an inspiration. Her patience with me, and with the frequent absences from home required by my work, has been truly amazing!

For nearly thirty years now, with Sharon's active encouragement, I have been trying to pass on to others something of the Catholic faith that my parents gave me and that the monks of Saint Meinrad helped me claim as my own. I have done this in two ways: 1) By writing about the Christian life (especially about the theology and practice of stewardship), and 2) By helping dioceses, parishes, schools, seminaries, religious communities and other Catholic organizations plan for the future, communicate effectively, and develop the human and financial resources they need to carry out the Church's mission. I have been incredibly blessed in my work, and I am deeply grateful for the opportunities given to me by my employer, RSI Catholic Services Group, to work closely with the dedicated and caring people who do the work of the Church on a daily basis.

But my first responsibility as a Christian called to share his faith is to hand on this great gift to my five children (ages 26-18). My kids are like I was many years ago. They are in the midst of an Augustinian struggle. They question, argue, debate, and try to dismiss the faith that their mother and I hold so dearly. They don't understand why we insist on going to Church at least once a week. They don't seem to appreciate how our faith keeps us going. How it allows us to handle deep disappointments. How it sustains us when things seems hopeless. And how it helps us survive when we're not sure we can handle the stress of daily living—our jobs, our family pressures, our financial worries, our aging parents, and all the worries that come with five adult-but-not-quite-independent children.

Some days I wish I could send all five of my children to Saint Meinrad. I wish I could enroll them in the School of Theology and expose them to the penetrating insights and profound wisdom of the Catholic Church. I wish they could come to know the monks of Saint Meinrad as I did—as ordinary men who struggle daily to be faithful to their vows and to grow in holiness. Wouldn't it be wonderful if they could experience Benedictine monasticism, "the school of the Lord's service," like I did? If only they could participate in the monks' prayer and work, the chant, the spiritual reading, and the wonderful liturgies. Perhaps they would discover there, as I did, the richness and the joy of life in Christ.

Of course, I can't live my children's lives or pack them off to a monastery. All Sharon and I can do is follow our parents' example and offer our children the faith that means so much to us. All we can do is share our faith with them.

With Sharon's strong encouragement, support, and assistance, I have written this little book of reflections on what Catholics believe, and how we are called to live as "stewards of joy." What is written here is dedicated with love to our children—Suzanne, Catherine, Margaret, Mary, and Dan. If nothing else, I sincerely hope that these reflections will help them understand why their mother and I feel so strongly about our Catholic faith.

So, with the help of God's grace, Sharon and I hope to pass our Catholic faith on to our children and to everyone who reads these words. That makes this little book truly a labor of love—freely undertaken out of gratitude to God for all his goodness to us.

That in all things God may be glorified through Jesus Christ, to whom belong glory and dominion forever and ever. Amen. (1 Peter 4:11)

Daniel Conway
August 15, 2006
The Assumption of the Blessed Virgin Mary

AUTHOR'S NOTE
WE BELIEVE

Throughout this little book of reflections you will encounter the expression, "we believe." It's important to identify who "we" are and what "believe" means to us.

In the first instance, "we" signifies my wife, Sharon, and me. We wish to share our faith with others—our children, first of all, and then with anyone else who reads this book. However, Sharon and I very much want to align ourselves with the faith of the Christian community, the Church. As a result we hope that the expression "we believe" describes more than just our personal beliefs. We want to speak with the Church and to articulate as best we can what all Catholic Christians believe, consistent with our primary reference, the *Catechism of the Catholic Church.*

Then there is the question of belief. When we say we believe something, we mean two things. First, we have opened ourselves in complete confidence and trust to something that we cannot know for certain by ordinary means. We believe because we trust those who tell us what we cannot know ourselves. Second, we place our integrity on the line when we say we believe something. In spite of our human weakness, which occasionally involves hesitation or doubt, we are certain that what we believe is true, and we stake our reputation on it. We stand behind what we say we believe.

So, for example, when we say that we believe God knows each one of us by name and loves us personally, as a loving father cares for his child, we are obviously not saying something that could be proven scientifically. We believe this because we have been told it by people we trust, and because we have opened ourselves to this wonderful mystery and have thus experienced for ourselves what it means. Is it really true that God knows each one of us by name and loves us personally as we are? We have our moments of doubt because we are human and because this claim—that the omnipotent God who made the universe knows me by name and loves me—is so outrageous! But, in the final analysis, we stand by this fantastic statement. We believe that it is certain and true.

Finally, for the purposes of this little book, I think it's important to say that we are called to be stewards of what we believe. Because faith is a gift from God, we have a responsibility to nurture and develop it and to share it generously with others. We believe that Christian faith is the source of true joy, of the satisfaction of our deepest desires as human persons. That's why we call this little book of reflections on what Catholic Christians believe, *Stewards of Joy: Taking Care Of and Sharing the Gift of Faith*.

INTRODUCTION
WE ARE CALLED TO BE STEWARDS OF JOY

The English writer C. S. Lewis described his conversion to Christianity as being "surprised by joy." Lewis had a very particular understanding of joy, which he carefully distinguished from both happiness and pleasure. Joy comes with the satisfaction of our deepest desires. Joy is what we long for always and rarely find. It is the experience of genuine unity and harmony with the world around us. It is the intimate connection with a person that makes us feel whole and complete as human beings.

The history of Christianity can be said to begin with joy—the greeting of the angel to the shepherds, "Be not afraid; for behold I bring you good news of a great joy" (Lk. 2:10). And, of course, the most profound experience of joy is found in the Easter mystery—Jesus' victory over sin and death in the Resurrection. Here the disciples on the road to Emmaus, and in Jerusalem and Galilee, encounter the Risen Lord and find their deepest longings fulfilled and their hearts burning within them.

The Oxford English Dictionary defines joy as "vivid pleasure arising from a sense of well-being or satisfaction." We might say that it is the opposite of restless anxiety or fear. Joy fills the emptiness in the pit of our stomachs. It causes us to feel that our unnamed fears are groundless. Joy counteracts our tendency to be constantly worried and depressed about the sad state of affairs the world has come to (again). Like the disciples on the road to Emmaus, like the saints throughout Christian history, like C. S. Lewis and countless other lost souls who are restless and filled with longing, joy takes us by surprise. We are amazed by the grace of God that comforts us and fills our hearts with peace.

Why, then, are so many of us Christians still lost? Why is there so much bitterness and anxiety among us? Why do we still feel desperate and afraid? Why do we bicker and quarrel among ourselves? Have we forgotten the hope we received at Christmas? Have we lost all sense of Easter joy?

In *The Joy of Full Surrender*, the great 19th century spiritual director, Father Jean-Pierre Caussade, writes, "There is nothing more free than a heart which sees only the life of God in the most deadly perils and troubles." This is the joy of martyrdom: to be completely confident in the presence and saving grace of God even in the most desperate and hopeless situations. As Father Caussade says: "The senses in terror, suddenly cry to the soul, Unhappy one! You have no resource left; you are lost! Instantly faith with a stronger voice answers: Keep firm, go forward and fear nothing!"

We believe that the fear and anxiety we Christians feel today stems from a lack of faith. Like the disciples, we fail to comprehend how God works in our world—bringing light into our darkness and healing into our brokenness. And we fail to listen for the "stronger voice of faith" among all the negative messages of doubt and despair in our world today.

Christians in the 21st century (as in every age) have been given the gift of joy. We have experienced, in a provisional way, what it means to be fully satisfied, to know lasting peace and to find true love. We are called to be stewards of the joy we have received in Christ—to nurture and develop it and to share it generously with others.

This little book of reflections, *Stewards of Joy: Taking Care Of and Sharing the Gift of Faith*, is intended to describe in a simple and straightforward way what we Catholics believe, and how we are called to live. The primary resource for this publication is the *Catechism of the Catholic Church*. If anything I have written is at odds with this "sure norm for the teaching of the faith" (as Pope John Paul II called it), then I am wrong—pure and simple. I have also relied on several works by Joseph Ratzinger (now Pope Benedict XVI) especially his *Introduction to Christianity*, which was the most powerful theological textbook I read during my years as a student at Saint Meinrad School of Theology. Finally, I am indebted to the distinguished theologian, Father Romano Guardini, for his insights into the struggle to live a Christian life as reflected in his wonderful book, *The Conversion of Augustine*.

In the words of Pope Benedict XVI, may this little book help all who read these reflections become better stewards of the Catholic faith: "May we never complain or be discouraged by life's trials. May the Lord help us to follow the path of love and, in submitting to its demands, find true joy."

CHAPTER ONE
GOD

God comes first. It seems strange to say, and it's very difficult to live, but this is what we believe. God comes before everything else. God is our first priority.

Who is this God? Why does he come first? (And why do we use the masculine personal pronoun "he" when talking about God?)

We believe that the world we live in—everything that exists from the vast, seemingly infinite universe to the smallest, most infinitesimal particle to those things that exist but are not material—was created by an intelligent, caring, and personal being who we call "God" (a very small name for someone so immense and incomprehensible). We also believe that the God who created the universe knows us personally and loves us—each and every one of us without exception—the way a loving father cares for his children. That's why we call God "he" even when we know that God is so much more than our understanding of male and female.

Sometimes people get the impression that God is an angry, judgmental being who likes to punish us for our sins. But this is not the God we believe in. We believe in the God who revealed himself to the Jews and who is made visible to us in Jesus Christ. This God is "slow to anger and rich in mercy." His patience is infinite. His forgiveness is freely given to all.

This does not mean that God doesn't care what we do or how we live. How could a loving father be indifferent to his children's decisions and actions? How could he not care whether we are living well or being truly happy?

No, the God we believe in cares deeply, but he does not force us to do anything. He does not compel us with lightning bolts from the sky. We have been given the gift of freedom. We can choose whatever we want and do whatever we like—as long as we are willing to accept the consequences. At the same time, God really does care about our choices, and he invites us (encourages us) to discover his will and to freely choose to live in ways that are pleasing to him—because they are good for us. We believe that there will come a day when we'll be asked to render an account of all our choices. Unless God is merciful, as we believe he is, that day could go badly for us all. We believe that it's our obligation to live well—according to God's plan for each of us—but we pray that we will be forgiven for the many ways that we have failed to live up to God's expectations as men and women called to make God known to others through what we say and do.

This is a wonderful image—a loving father-god who gives us freedom and forgives us when we make the wrong choices—but how do we know it's true? Why should this image of God be truer than those of ancient mythology like Zeus or Isis or Baal? How do we know that there is a God and, if there is one, what God is like?

Philosophers tell us that there are things we can know about God because we are intelligent and because it's reasonable to think that our universe was planned rather than accidental. Many of the contemporary arguments about evolution versus "creationism" or "intelligent design" represent the struggle to find appropriate ways to make the case for a planned, purposeful cause for our existence that goes beyond a random cosmic event without meaning or significance.

But beyond what we can discern through reason alone, we believe that we can know God personally, even intimately, in spite of the fact that he remains an incomprehensible mystery. We believe that we can know God because he has reached out to us and told us who he is. God has taken the initiative and communicated with us through his intervention in the history of the people of Israel and, most of all, through his self-revelation in the life, death, and resurrection of Jesus Christ, the incarnate word of God. With the ancient Jews from the time of Abraham onward, we believe that God has revealed himself to us in the tradition and the writings of the Jewish people. With the apostles and the consistent testimony of Christians during the past 2000 years, we believe that Jesus Christ is God-made-man, the only son of God who was born in a stable in Bethlehem. He lived and worked as an ordinary human being for most of his life, eventually served as a teacher, healer and miracle worker, suffered and died for our sake and then rose again to new life to show us that love is stronger than death.

We believe this. We take it seriously. We try to understand its meaning for us. We long to share this belief with others because we know that it makes a difference in the way we live. We can't prove this is true the way a historian verifies something that happened long ago, or the way a scientist proves a hypothesis, or the way a mathematician solves a long and complicated equation. We believe that we can know God because we trust the people who have shared their faith with us and because we have opened ourselves to him and allowed him to come into our lives. We can know, love, and serve God because he has first loved us and revealed himself to us. That's the whole meaning of the Bible and of Christian tradition. It's a simple article of faith that changes our whole understanding of the world and of ourselves.

We believe that God is not a fantasy or a stranger or an angry, uncaring life force. God is love. God's love reaches out to us, cares about us, and rescues us the way a loving father would. God is also our brother, Jesus Christ, who lived as we live and who died to set us free. God is the unseen Holy Spirit who works silently in our lives, and in our world, to make things better and to bring unity, peace, and harmony to an angry, divided, and unhappy world.

This is the mystery of the Holy Trinity that we believe even though we don't understand it. We believe that God is a community of three persons that preserves the individuality of each. God is what each of us (and all of creation) longs for—an experience of perfect unity or connectedness that does not destroy our individual identity or uniqueness. We want what God is. We want to be like God because we were made in his image and likeness. We want knowledge, love, and communion. We want joy: the satisfaction of our deepest desires. We want peace: the resolution of all conflict and anxiety.

We want to be united with God, and, until that day comes, we will never be fully satisfied. We can (and often do) search for the satisfaction of our deepest desires in a variety of places that promise what they can't deliver. But as St. Augustine said so clearly from his own profound experience, "Our hearts are restless till they rest in you, O God."

We believe in God, but unless we put God first in our lives, nothing can satisfy us. That's why so many of us, believers and unbelievers alike, live restless, anxious lives. We are filled with desires that we can't satisfy. We long for love, for success, for happiness, or for peace, but we can't find them. We will never find what we are looking for as long as something other than God occupies first place in our lives.

God comes first. We believe this. With the help of God's grace, we try to live it as best we can. And it makes a huge difference in our daily lives.

Prayer

Loving Father, thank you for the gift of your love. You have given us life. You have reached out to us and invited us to know you, love you, and serve you. May we respond to your gifts generously by sharing your love and by seeking to do your will. May we find in you the joy our souls yearn for, and may we learn to be faithful stewards of this joy in everything we do. Amen.

Questions for Reflection and Discussion

Does God really come first in my life? Or do I have other priorities—relationships, work, possessions, self-interest? How would my life be different if God really came first?

What is my image of God—an angry, judgmental figure or a loving parent or friend who knows me by name and cares deeply about what I do?

How do we know that God is love? What evidence, or experiences, would lead us to believe that love is the essence of who God is?

What do you long for in your heart of hearts? How would placing God first help you to find happiness, satisfaction, or peace?

CHAPTER TWO
JESUS CHRIST

Jesus Christ is the meaning of the world and of my life. There is no one more important to me personally, or to all of humanity, than Jesus Christ. That's why his name is revered above all other names. More than Mozart or Michelangelo or Alexander. More than Caesar or Napoleon or Abraham Lincoln. More than Buddha or Moses or Mohammed or Confucius. More than the Dali Lama or Billy Graham or Pope Bendict XVI. The name of Jesus is worthy of reverence, respect, and adoration. It is a sacred name, a name that contains the key to the mystery of God and the mystery of man.

We believe in Jesus Christ, and we worship him as true God and true man. What is so special about this man, Jesus? Why is he worthy of our total devotion? Why do we choose to follow him above all others?

We believe that Jesus Christ is God's gift-of-self to us. Jesus is God incarnate, God in our flesh and blood. The Christmas story announces to all the world the joyful news that God is with us (Emmanuel). He is one with us. He has renounced his omnipotent power and become the most vulnerable of creatures—a baby, an innocent, vulnerable, and totally dependent human being. The God who made the universe, who knows everything and can do anything, has been handed over to the care of two ordinary human beings, his mother, Mary, and her husband, Joseph. He has allowed himself to be fed and clothed and bathed and changed by them. He has given them complete authority over him until the proper time comes. Then he will hand himself over to a much less benign authority, the ruling classes of Israel and of Rome.

Why would God do this? And, assuming it's true, why is it so important for my life and for the history of the world?

We believe that God loves us so much that he sent his only son to save us. Save us from what? From our brokenness. From our unhappiness. From our inhumanity. From our suffering. From our sin. How does Jesus Christ, true God and true man, save us from ourselves and from the sins of the world?

God becomes one of us. He lives as we live. He suffers as we suffer. And he dies most cruelly on the Cross. St. Paul tells us that because he has "emptied himself, taking the form of a servant,…God has highly exalted him and bestowed on him the name which is above every name, that at the name of Jesus every knee should bow…and every tongue confess that Jesus Christ is Lord, to the glory of God the Father" (Phil 2:7-10). Jesus saves us by showing us with his words and his life that self-surrender and living for others is what life is all about. It is the only way to live free and be happy. It is the only way to escape the depression and anxiety of daily life. It is the only hope we have of being truly fulfilled and "successful" as human beings. We must surrender our self-will and self-centeredness and give ourselves freely and fully to God and to others. In other words, we must take up our crosses and follow Jesus through death to eternal life.

This is hard news. Surrender? Take up our crosses? Live for others and not for ourselves? This is not what we want to hear. It is not what the world tells us. It is not the good life, or the lifestyles of the rich and famous. It's not the road to success or even to happiness as most of us understand happiness. It's a totally different way of life, a countercultural way. Most of us aren't very good at it—even when we've committed ourselves to living this way. We want to follow Jesus, but everything inside us, and all around us, seems to get in the way.

What difference does belief in Jesus Christ make—practically, concretely? To the extent that we know him personally and resolve to follow him wholeheartedly, Jesus Christ has a profound impact on our daily lives. He transforms us from self-centered individuals whose primary goal in life is to satisfy our own needs and desires. He transforms us into people who can surrender our own interests for the sake of others (for the common good) and who find meaning and purpose in things beyond ourselves—in marriage and family life; in friendship and community service; in work that expresses our human dignity and makes our world a little better; in artistic, athletic, and cultural experiences that celebrate the highest human achievements; and in worship that lifts our minds and hearts to God.

Is it absolutely necessary to know Jesus Christ, to have a personal relationship with him, in order to be happy, joyous, and free? Aren't there millions of people who don't know Christ and yet live reasonably unselfish, contented and productive lives?

Yes, of course. But we believe that every human being deserves the chance to come to know Jesus Christ as the meaning of human existence and as the one who reveals to us the mystery of God. In fact, we are not primarily interested in introducing Jesus to people as someone who lived in the past and did great things. The Gospels are the living record of an encounter with Jesus that has past, present, and future dimensions.

On the basis of our own experience, and the testimony of countless Christians during the past 2,000 years, we believe that there is nothing more satisfying—mentally, physically, or spiritually—than the opportunity to know, love, and serve Jesus Christ now! A personal encounter with Jesus can happen many ways, but the traditional ways to come to know Jesus – here and now – are through prayer, holy reading, the sacraments (especially the Eucharist) and service to others. As stewards of the joy that comes from knowing Jesus Christ, we want to share this experience with everyone. We want everyone to come to know Jesus by their own free choice, and so we believe it is our obligation, as well as our joy, to share our faith with others whenever and wherever we can.

This commitment to share our faith with others does not make us fanatics. While we may respect those whose Christian witness is bolder and more enthusiastic than ours, we believe that living our faith one day at a time is the most profound form of evangelization. We hope to introduce others to Christ by following him, by taking to heart his words and his example, and by using the opportunities that God gives us to share with others the profound joy we have experienced in Jesus' name.

Unfortunately, the name of Jesus Christ has lost much of its power and significance in our contemporary society. Too often it is a name that is either abused or treated with indifference. Even those of us who claim to be his disciples too often fail to live as witnesses to the sacred power of his holy name. This is very sad. Although we believe that Jesus Christ is the meaning of the world and of each individual person, we too often act as if other things claimed our primary allegiance.

The Scriptures tell us that Jesus himself was tempted to live differently—to demonstrate his divine power, to look to his own comfort, and to avoid the suffering and humiliation that were his human destiny. Jesus resisted these temptations. He freely chose to be a man for others and to set aside his own immediate needs and desires for our sake and for the sake of God's kingdom which is here in our midst and, at the same time, still to come.

We are aware that these statements of our Christian faith can sound outrageous to those who do not believe. If our faith in Jesus Christ sounds strange to you, if it strikes you as a weird way of understanding the world and our place in it, you are not alone. St. Paul observed that faith in Jesus Christ was a scandal—a stumbling block—to the Jews whose reverence for God did not seem to allow for the possibility of a God-man. And it was foolishness to the Greeks whose wisdom and philosophy had already established that if there is a God he is very distant and removed from us. We don't pretend that our Catholic way of life is easy to understand or to live. But we believe that it is true. And because it's true, we believe that it shows us the way to be happy, joyous and free. If only we can surrender our willful self-centeredness and allow the grace of God to enter our hearts and set us free. Then we will live in Christ and know true joy.

If you want what we have, we invite you to look to Jesus and let him set you free. If you do, we believe you will discover for yourself what we mean when we pray with Pope Benedict XVI, "Lord, Jesus Christ, you are the meaning of the world and of my life. Amen."

Prayer

Lord Jesus Christ, help me to meet you face-to-face in prayer, in the Eucharist, in sacred reading, and in loving service to others. Help me to recognize you in strangers and in those who are closest to me every day. Help me to follow your teaching, to imitate you in all my actions, and to love you with an open, joyful heart. Lord Jesus, I believe that you are the meaning of my life. Help my unbelief. Sustain me in my struggles and fears. Support me when I stumble and fall. Support me with your love and your hope. May I always have the courage and the strength to take up my cross and follow you. And may I always say, "Thank you" no matter

✠

what the circumstances of my life. I love you, Lord Jesus. You are the meaning of the world and of my life. Amen.

Questions for Reflection and Discussion

Who is Jesus Christ? Do I have a personal relationship with him—or is he simply a remote historical or religious figure?

Is it possible to know him, love him, and serve him in an intimate and personal way? How does knowing Jesus help us to know ourselves? How does it change the way we relate to others—and to our world?

What if Christian faith is true? What difference does it make in our daily lives and in the way we experience the world we live in?

What does it mean to say that Jesus is true God and true man? What does it mean to encounter him in the sacrament of the Eucharist and to receive Him—Body and Blood, Soul and Divinity?

If Jesus' resurrection from the dead is a real event that liberated all of us from the power of sin and death, how does this change our lives? How should we respond to this amazing, mind-blowing miracle of God's grace?

CHAPTER THREE
CHURCH

Going to Church is the most important thing we do each week. We believe it is so important because Church is an integral part of who we are. It is not something extra—like a social club we belong to or a group we've joined for a particular purpose. We believe that the Church is the family of God and that our baptism as Christians makes us family members with all the rights and responsibilities of God's children, of brothers and sisters in Christ. We go to Church each week on the Lord's Day to be united with Christ in the Sunday Eucharist and to join with our sisters and brothers throughout the world in expressing our profound gratitude for all that God has given us.

In the previous chapter we talked about the joy of coming to know Jesus Christ personally—here and now. The Church makes this encounter possible. As the Body of Christ, the Church is where we meet Christ, where we unite with him, and where we share in his life in a profoundly intimate and personal way. The Second Vatican Council speaks of the Church as the sacrament of our encounter with Christ. This means the Church is both a sign of our communion with God in Christ and an active agent of change that through the miracle of God's grace is working to bring about this encounter.

We go to Church because we meet Jesus there—in the scriptures, in the Eucharist and all the sacraments, in fellowship with other Christians, and in service to those in need.

The Church that we love has had its ups and downs in the 2,000 years of Christian history. It has served as home to countless saints—women and men of great holiness and integrity who have made a real difference in the world through their service to others as teachers, healers, counselors, political leaders, pastors, popes, and prophets. All these wonderful people, including those we know are saints and many others whose lives of holiness are hidden from us, loved the Church. All of them dedicated their lives to following Christ and worshiping him in the Eucharist, Christ's amazing gift-of-self to us. There are many saints we could list here—beginning with Mary, Joseph and all the apostles and continuing down through the ages to women and men of our own day like Blessed Teresa of Calcutta and Pope John Paul II. These are people who have

✠

inspired us, who have shared their faith with us, and who have showed us how to follow Christ in the world as we know it—here and now.

Various eras of Christian history have also witnessed thoroughly corrupt popes, bishops, and priests. And every age has known its share of Catholic men and women who are indifferent or even hostile to the teaching and practice of the Church. Our recent history has called our attention to the sexual perversions of a small number of priests who managed to do great damage to children and youth. It has also shown that many of the bishops failed to understand the seriousness of the problem and that the responses of some were woefully inadequate and inappropriate. The family of God is made up of sinners as well as saints, and one of the great mysteries of our faith is the fact that the Church survives as Christ promised it would, in spite of the faults and failings of its members—including us.

Christian history is filled with examples of great things that have been inspired by the Church—from magnificent architecture, art, and music to profound intellectual achievements and outstanding educational institutions to service organizations dedicated to extraordinary acts of charity and unselfishness. We believe that in every era, no matter how bleak things may appear, the sins of Church members are countered by a genuine outpouring of faith, hope, and love that shows the Church to be alive and young. The Church is resilient. It dies with its Lord—weighed down by the heavy burden of our sinfulness—and it rises again with him buoyed up by the presence and power of the Holy Spirit.

We believe that the Church is our point of connection with all men and women, the living and the dead. As the family of God, the Church transcends both time and space. It unites us with all those who have gone before us—including those family members who have died and who are now united with Christ in the communion of the saints. Because we are all destined to be united in Christ, we are confident that, one day, we will all be together again in the unity and peace of God's kingdom. This is not just wishful thinking. It is a profound hope that springs from our conviction that we human beings were not meant to live and die alone or to be forever cut off from those who are most dear to us. We believe that we will all be united in heaven on the last day—when "every tear will be wiped away" and when we will all experience great joy.

This is why we believe that going to Church is the most important thing we do each week. Even if we don't feel like it. Even if we don't get much out of a particular homily or liturgical celebration. The Eucharist is always a precious, undeserved gift. It is our means of experiencing communion with Christ and with the other members of his body. We want to participate in this divine action even when we don't want to. We believe that we need the grace of the sacraments, and the inspiration of God's Word, to live freely and to be happy even when we don't feel like it.

That's why the Church means so much to us, and why we take the liturgy and the sacraments so seriously. We believe that the Church, as the living Body of Christ and the one family of God, is the source of our most profound joys—both now and in the world to come. We love the Church and we wish that everyone could share in this joy. As stewards of this joy, we accept the challenge to preserve and strengthen the Church. And we gladly share this great gift with others.

Prayer

Holy Spirit of God, on the day of Pentecost you gathered the weak and troubled disciples and transformed them into a bold and courageous community of faith, the Church. Help us to be faithful members of the Body of Christ. Teach us to speak with confidence and hope and to bear witness in our lives to the miracle of God's grace among us. Unite us with Christ and with one another so that the Church we love may grow in holiness and one day achieve its divine mission: to establish the kingdom of Christ and of God here on earth. Amen.

Questions for Reflection and Discussion

Why is Church such an important part of our lives? Isn't Christian faith something personal and private? Why do we need the Church?

How does the Church make it possible for us to encounter Christ in a profound and personal way? What role do the sacraments, especially the Eucharist, play in our journey to Christ?

For nearly two thousand years, the Church has been the home of both saints and sinners. How does the sinful humanity of the Church's members, and the scandals caused by many of her leaders, correlate with the Church's holiness and her divine mission?

How does the Church connect us with all those who have gone before us (the communion of saints)? What's the relationship between the Church and the kingdom of God that is both here and now and still to come?

Chapter Four
Family

God comes first, then family. There is nothing more important in this world than our family—not careers, not fame or fortune, not politics or sports or the arts. Family is the first and most fundamental unit of society. It is a gift from God that we should treasure, cultivate, and defend when necessary.

Family gives us our most basic identity and role in society. I am Dan Conway, son of Jack and Helen, husband of Sharon, father of Suzanne, Catherine, Margaret, Mary, and Dan. Although my work takes me outside my family and gives me a social identity that is broader than my role in the family, my work is not who I am. It is what I do for the sake of my family, first of all, and then to fulfill my obligations to society and to the Church.

Love and respect are the preeminent family values. We believe that every family member is equal in dignity—from the oldest grandparent to the child in the womb. Each family member has his or her special needs. The family exists to respond to these individual needs but also to remind us that we are not alone. Family helps us recognize that we are called to share and to sacrifice, when necessary, for the sake of the greater good and the needs of the family as a whole.

Every family experiences tension and disagreement. Human persons living closely together are bound to get on each other's nerves, to see things differently, even to form very different opinions about the things that we value most. Strong families accommodate different personalities and divergent points of view. They also establish core values that every family member is asked to respect. If an individual steps out of bounds and violates one or more of our most basic beliefs and values, a good family does not reject him or her. Love and respect remain—above all else. This does not mean that anything goes—or that we accept or approve of everything that our family members say or do. Sometimes it's necessary to state clearly our disapproval and our inability to accept certain behaviors. But this does not cause us to abandon individual family members or to disrespect their fundamental dignity as children of God or as members of our family.

We believe that patriotism, the love of our country, flows directly from the love and respect we experience in our families. Nations are not absolutes or ends in themselves. They exist for the sake of the individuals, families, and communities that are joined together along geographic, historic, and cultural lines (in freedom and under the rule of law) for the sake of the common good. To love and respect our country, to work for it and defend it when necessary, is a great privilege and a serious responsibility.

We believe that our country, the United States of America, is a wonderful place to live and work and raise a family. Our ancestors chose to come here—often at great personal sacrifice. They helped build this country. They fought for it, and, in some cases, they died for it. We owe our nation the honor it deserves out of respect for our ancestors but also for the sake of our children and grandchildren who will inherit this country with all its strengths and weaknesses.

Because of the love and respect we have for our country, we believe we have an obligation to speak out, and to act, whenever our leaders fail to govern responsibly. In our lifetime (from the second half of the 20th century to the present), we have witnessed various instances of irresponsible government. These include the Vietnam War, the Watergate scandal, the tragic Supreme Court decision in *Roe v. Wade*, and the continuing inability of the richest nation in the world to deal effectively with poverty, homelessness, and the absence of adequate health care for millions of Americans.

We have also witnessed the demise of Communism, the growth of terrorism, and the inability of the international community to work together to guarantee peace and prosperity in all regions of the world—especially the poorest and most underdeveloped nations. The love and respect that we have for our nation does not cause us to be blind to its problems or to ignore its many faults and failings. On the contrary, the more we love our country, the more we must work to make it better!

Family life in the United States and in many other parts of the world is increasingly threatened by the growing divorce rate and by major shifts in our economic, demographic, and cultural makeup. We believe that this is a serious matter that requires much greater attention and leadership from all of us, especially our elected officials. Unless the family is clearly recognized for what it is—the most fundamental element in our social structure—we risk weakening our society at its core and undermining our most basic human and social values.

We believe the family is too important to take for granted. As stewards of all the good things God has given us, we have a special responsibility to nurture, to care for and to share this most precious gift. That's why we look to Mary, Joseph, and Jesus, the Holy Family, as a source of inspiration and as a model for contemporary family life. Their love and respect for one another, their generous service to all who were in need, and their complete openness to God's will for them no matter what sacrifices it required, should be a challenge and encouragement to all of us who love our families and want to make them the very best that they can be.

Prayer

Lord Jesus Christ, you chose to come among us as a dependent child subject to the loving care of Mary and Joseph. Most of your brief time on earth was spent living as a member of the Holy Family—growing in wisdom, age, and grace in the ordinary circumstances of daily life. Teach us to recognize the importance of family life, to nurture and protect this most basic and important unit of human society. Help us to celebrate the family as our first experience of you and of your body, the domestic church. May our families always nurture and sustain the great gift of life. May they grow in holiness and in courageous witness to the truth. Through the intercession of your mother, the Blessed Virgin Mary, and St. Joseph, the man who was chosen to be your special guardian, may we learn to know you, love you, and serve you. May our families grow in holiness and in hope in your name. Amen.

Questions for Reflection and Discussion

"God comes first, then family." Do you agree with this statement? Why is it so important today?

How do families teach love and respect? How do they form individuals for life in society? For membership in the one family of God, the Church?

What's the right relationship between family values and patriotism? Between family and Church?

What are the main threats to family life today? How can we work to overcome them—with the help of God's grace?

CHAPTER FIVE
LIFE

Human life is sacred. It is a gift from God so precious that no one has the right to take it away. "We are stewards, not owners, of the life God has entrusted to us. It is not ours to dispose of" (*Catechism of the Catholic Church* #2280).

Since the beginning of history, human beings have violated this most basic law of God: Thou shalt not kill. The Bible records the story of Cain and Abel as the first instance of man's inhumanity against man. What began with one brother's jealous rage has continued—sometimes on a massive scale—to our present day. Anger and envy are at the heart of human conflict—from minor family quarrels to deadly warfare among nations and peoples.

We believe that the sanctity of human life is absolute. It is written in our hearts as a law that may never be violated without severe consequences to individuals, families and societies. A society that does not respect life is not a true human community. It suffers from a grave misunderstanding of who we are as children of God. It fails to uphold the stewardship responsibility we have to nurture, protect, and develop this most precious gift of God, the gift of life itself.

Simply "to be" is a great miracle, a wondrous undeserved blessing. None of us has the right to exist. We are a gifted people. God's grace, the outpouring of his creative love, brings us into being. Once we have been given life by God, at the moment of our conception, we are also given the dignity that belongs inalienably to every human person. We are, therefore, worthy of the courtesy and respect due every child of God. This is true of everyone—from the most talented and gifted among us to those on the margins of society who seem most useless or debased.

No matter who we are, no matter what we have done, no matter what has happened to us, no one can take from us our fundamental human dignity. No one has the right to deny us the life that God has so lovingly given us. We believe this with all our minds and hearts. It is absolutely fundamental to who we are and what we believe as members of the one family of God.

Individuals, families and societies are called to celebrate life and to do everything possible to develop and to promote what Pope John Paul II called the "culture of life." Government has the obligation to nurture and to defend human life. In contemporary American society, this means outlawing all forms of direct abortion and assisted suicide. It also means abolishing capital punishment. In addition, as responsible citizens, we must hold our local, state and federal governments accountable for controlling crime, the drug trade, pornography, prostitution and all other activities (including various ill-considered social policies) that degrade human beings and threaten the welfare of local communities and our nation as a whole.

We believe that each human person has a responsibility to promote life. We begin with ourselves—with our health and our own lifestyles. Do we exercise, eat right, get proper medical care? Do we drink too much, smoke, or abuse drugs? Do we gamble excessively or spend too much time partying? Have we spoken out or taken appropriate action against the evils of abortion, assisted suicide, and capital punishment? Are we working to promote peace and justice here at home and throughout the world? Do we live lives that show reverence for the life God has given us, or are we the unwitting participants in the growing culture of death—or as Pope Benedict XVI calls it, the "anti-culture of death"?

We believe that each of us will be asked to render an account of our stewardship of the gift of life. What will be the outcome? In the Gospels, Jesus speaks some of his harshest words to those hypocrites who scandalously lead others to the realm of "living death." We believe in the infinite mercy of God, but we also know that grave sins against life are impossible to reverse—whether it is the death of one person by murder, abortion, or suicide, or the catastrophic destruction of entire cities by war, famine, or genocide. We do not want these grave sins on our conscience—either because of what we have done or what we have failed to do.

We believe that the major sins against life have their roots in smaller sins—anger, jealousy, bickering, gossip, and prejudice of all kinds. To uphold the dignity of life means to give every human being his or her full respect in all situations and circumstances. This is not an easy task given our human tendency to quarrel, criticize, and cut down others (especially those who are different from us). However, we believe that a profound respect for the life of every person is essential if we are ever to end the vicious cycle of hatred and violence that has produced so much death and destruction throughout human history right down to our present day.

The commandment to respect life and keep it sacred is absolute. It maintains our basic humanity, and it reminds who we are as children of God and sisters and brothers to all. We pray that the Lord of Life, who is also the Prince of Peace, will inspire us with his gentle strength to resist the culture of death wherever it appears and to always choose life!

Prayer

God, the author of all life, help us to nurture and protect this most precious gift. Help us to recognize and defend the dignity of all human life—from the moment of conception until the time you have chosen for our death. Guard us against all temptations to be angry or disrespectful. Deliver us from the evils of hatred and violence in all their many forms. Above all, help us to see your face in our sisters and brothers whoever they are and wherever they may be. Make us women and men who love peace and who are ready to work for liberty and justice for all. Amen.

Questions for Reflection and Discussion

What does it mean to be "stewards, not owners" of the life God has given us? How can we nurture and share this most precious gift of life?

What does it mean to say that the sanctity of human life is absolute? Aren't there legitimate exceptions to this principle? When is it OK to take someone else's life?

What do you think Pope John Paul II meant when he talked about the "culture of life"? Can you describe what a life-giving culture is like? How about its opposite: a culture (or anti-culture) of death?

How do major sins against life develop from smaller sins? How can we prevent the progressive spread of anger and violence?

CHAPTER SIX
HUMAN SEXUALITY

Sex is for marriage. Today, this is probably the most countercultural (and therefore most controversial) Catholic teaching, but we believe it is absolutely true. In fact, the more we observe the actual results of the so-called sexual revolution, the more firmly we believe that the Catholic Church has "got it right" when it comes to human sexuality. We are aware that not everyone agrees with us on this, including many Catholics, but we stand by our convictions.

Human sexuality is a gift from God that affects all aspects of the human person: body, mind, emotions, and spirituality. Sex can be a powerful creative force. It can also cause great harm. Sex is good, and sexual sins are all misuses or perversions of something good—the life-giving, creative energy that God has hard-wired into our human personalities. One of the primary challenges of human life is to channel our sexual energy toward what is good and away from what is hurtful or destructive to ourselves and to others.

The marriage of a man and a woman places sexuality in its proper perspective. It provides a context of loving, permanent commitment. It makes it possible for a man and a woman "to become one flesh," to enter into a form of personal communion that frees them from loneliness and that commits them to a lifelong partnership as collaborators with God in the work of creation. We believe that a husband and wife are gifts to one another. Equal in dignity and in their respective rights and responsibilities, married persons complement and perfect one another. United as one flesh, they are sacramental signs of the communion with God that we are all called to experience as human beings made in God's image and likeness. Married couples are stewards of the gifts they are to each other. They are called to nurture and develop the unity they possess as loving partners. And they are called to share their love generously with others—especially their children—out of gratitude for the many gifts they have received from the God who is love.

Sex is for marriage, and marriage is for unity between the spouses and for children. The two basic purposes of human sexuality—to unite a man and a woman in marriage and to collaborate with God in the creation of new life—are inseparable. They are the two integral dimensions of the mystery of sexuality, and these two dimensions constantly support and sustain one another during the course of a couple's married life together.

We don't pretend that it's easy to achieve the kind of integration or self-mastery that mature men and women are called to develop as stewards of this great gift from God. As the Church teaches, developing a mature sexuality is the work of a lifetime. It faces new challenges as our individual circumstances change, and it requires renewed efforts at different stages of life. Sex can be a source of great joy. It can also cause profound disappointment or frustration if we are not able to handle it maturely.

There are strong voices in our contemporary culture that proclaim the "right" of consenting adults to engage in all forms of sexual activity "so long as no one gets hurt." We don't try to impose our beliefs on others, and we certainly don't judge those whose convictions are different from ours. But we think the evidence is overwhelming that there is no such thing as "free love" and that casual, or recreational, sex is destructive of human persons and of our society as a whole. The way sex is cheaply used in advertising, in entertainment, and in the recreational activities of young and old alike does not build up the human community. We believe that our society trivializes marriage and family life. It degrades individuals (especially women) and turns them into sex objects. In the end, we believe that the erotic anti-culture we live in today makes us less than we are called to be as individuals and as a loving, generous, and productive society.

Jewish and Christian tradition single out *adultery* as a grave sin. This is because it violates the exclusive covenant between a man and a woman in marriage. Extramarital sex causes deep and lasting harm to spouses, to children and to society as a whole. We believe that forgiveness should be the response to all sins against the marriage vows, but we also know how difficult this can be and how much damage is done when a husband or wife is unfaithful.

In our society there is a lot of pressure on us to accept homosexual relationships as normal. The main argument is that people do not choose their sexual orientation and those who find themselves attracted to people of the same sex should have the opportunity to enter into exclusive relationships or "same-sex marriages" that can satisfy their need for companionship and sexual expression.

We disagree—not because we fear (or are repulsed by) homosexuality, but because we believe that same-sex relationships contradict the basic purposes of human sexuality. The physical (and emotional) complementarity of male and female sexuality, and the openness to procreation, are not incidental but integral to what sex is all about. As we see it, sex only makes sense when experienced by a married man and woman. Outside of marriage sex can give pleasure, and it can imitate the quest for unity that is at the heart of humanity's search for love, but it can't be truly life-giving. As always, we have no wish to judge others. We are stating—as clearly and positively as we can—what we believe to be true. We know that we will be held accountable only for our own self-mastery and for our fidelity to the vocation God has given us.

Other sexual sins are more or less serious depending on who is involved and what the consequences are. Incest, child abuse, rape, prostitution, and pornography are among the most destructive abuses of human sexuality. Even in marriage, it is possible to abuse the dignity of a spouse by regarding him or her as an object or by forcing another to engage in activities that are personally degrading. Healthy sexuality takes work, but we believe it is a blessing from God to be appreciated and enjoyed for the good thing that it is!

In the end, we believe that the Church is right when it teaches that marriage between a man and a woman is the only really appropriate place for sexual activity. We want to affirm this truth as we understand it and to thank God for this wonderful gift of sexuality—especially as we have experienced it in our marriage and family life.

Prayer

God of love, you have given us the great gift of sexuality. You have blessed married couples with the exchange of physical intimacy to unite a man and woman as one flesh and to share with them your creative power. Help us to treasure this gift and to use it wisely—for our own good and for the good of humanity. Help us to be intimate, playful and life-giving in all our relationships. Make us chaste and loving in all our thoughts, words and actions. O God, you know how we struggle to be responsible stewards of our relationships and our sexuality. Grant us the grace to be faithful and unselfish in all that we do in this vitally important but often challenging area of our lives. Amen.

Questions for Reflection and Discussion

Do you agree that "sex is for marriage"? Why or why not?

How is Church teaching on human sexuality countercultural?

How do the failings of Church leaders (and all human beings) affect our ability to understand, and practice, what we believe about sex?

Is it possible to uphold the Christian view of human sexuality without judging those who don't share this view? What are some of the challenges we face as we attempt to live these values on a daily basis?

CHAPTER SEVEN
MONEY

"The love of money is the root of all evils; it is through this craving that some have wandered away from the faith and pierced their hearts with many pangs" (1 Tm. 6:10).

As St. Paul points out, an inordinate desire or craving for money or material things is at the core of all our troubles. It is the root of all evil. It tempts us all to wander from our true selves, from what we know is right and true, and from the God who alone deserves our wholehearted longing and desire.

Most of us are not obsessed with money in an extreme, pathological way. We are not King Midas or Ebenezer Scrooge, a robber baron or an oil tycoon. And yet, this craving that St. Paul talks about infects us all. We *are* obsessed with material things—the basics that we know we must have (food, shelter, clothing, health care) and the extras that we have come to regard as symbols of our status in the world (cars, computers, widescreen TV sets, the latest fashions, and much more). We cling to whatever wealth and property we have because we are afraid of losing our security, our independence, and our self-respect. We want to be people of means because we know that the world can be a cruel place, and we feel that we need all the weapons (the material resources) we can muster to survive and to flourish in a world that measures success and happiness by how much we possess.

We believe that this preoccupation with money and material things is a serious problem for us as individuals, as families and as a society. It gnaws at the fabric of our culture and makes us spiritually ragged and weak. It inverts our values to the point where material things and appearances, such as status and prestige, become far more important than personal relationships or spiritual values. In 21st century America, the craving, the cupidity, St. Paul speaks about has become deeply embedded into our culture. It is part of the air we breathe as a materialistic, consumer-oriented society. Advertising and the entertainment media help form our cultural values. Therein we are constantly urged to acquire, consume, and dispose of large quantities of material things. We are taught to see ourselves as consumers who must earn more and more in order to spend more and more. The cycle is vicious and unending. The more we have, the more we think we need *ad infinitum*.

To break out of this self-destructive pattern, and to be free from the obsessive desire for more money and material things, we must come to see ourselves as stewards. We must recognize that God alone is the owner of the goods of the earth. All that we have (and all that we are) comes from God as a free and undeserved gift. Although we believe in the right to own and use property as individuals in a free society, we acknowledge that, in reality, we are merely stewards of what truly belongs to God. As stewards, we are called to cultivate and develop what has been given to us—and to share it generously with others out of justice and love. But as stewards we also renounce all claims to "absolute ownership" and we seek to discern God's will for the development and use of the gifts he has entrusted to our care.

Beyond this basic understanding of stewardship, we have a further obligation as baptized Christians who seek to follow Jesus Christ. In the Gospels, the Lord issues a radical invitation to those who wish to follow him: "Go, sell what you have, and give to the poor;…and come, follow me" (Mk. 10:21; cf. Mt. 19:16-24; Lk. 18:18-25). What does this mean for us—ordinary people who wish to follow Jesus as the way to happiness and peace? Most of us cannot follow the Lord's instructions literally. We have families and obligations to ourselves and others that make this impossible. How do we accept the Lord's invitation to let go of everything we have and trust in him completely?

Letting go is not something we do willingly or easily. We are taught that surrender means defeat. We are afraid of what might happen to us if we let go. What will others think if we give up our social status? What if we end up needing the money that we are asked to share with the poor or with the mission of the Church? Doesn't letting go mean losing control? Doesn't it force us to settle for less than we want or deserve?

Letting go is what Jesus did when he became man. When he was born into poverty and homelessness. When he lived quietly among the people of Nazareth and learned a trade. When he was baptized by John and began the life of an itinerant preacher and healer. When he chose twelve very ordinary men to lead his Church. When he accepted the Father's will and agreed to suffer and die for our sins. When he embraced death and opened to all the gates of eternal life. When he sent the Holy Spirit to inspire us and to give us the courage to let go whenever we are stuck in our sins.

Letting go is what disciples of Jesus Christ are called to do when they are challenged to acknowledge that everything they have (and everything they are) they received as a free gift from God. We cannot hold or grasp the things that belong to God. We can only care for them as grateful and responsible stewards who share them generously with others and, ultimately, give them back again to God with increase. Christian disciples cling to God by letting go of all the stuff that separates them from God's grace. They open their hearts to God by being good and faithful stewards of all God's gifts.

Most of us cannot literally "sell everything we have and give it to the poor," but we can make letting go of our obsession with money and material things a powerful, positive expression of what it means to follow in the footsteps of the Lord "who, though he was in the form of God, did not regard equality with God something to be grasped" (Phil. 2:6). When we let go, as he did, we become simpler, poorer (in the eyes of the world), more generous and much less self-centered. We become like Christ. This is the first principle of Christian spirituality: to imitate Christ by emptying ourselves, by living as he did, and by clinging to him alone.

This attitude or mindset is light years removed from the cravings we experience when we are obsessed with money and material things. It is also far removed from the feelings of frustration and despair that accompany the vicious cycle of earning, spending, and incurring debt that have become such an integral part of our materialistic culture.

In the Old Testament, the Jewish people were given the Commandment: Thou shall not steal. As always, Jesus affirms the wisdom of the old law but he takes it a step further and makes it new. "Seek first the kingdom of God and his righteousness, and all these things will be given you" (Mt. 6:33).

We don't pretend that we have been very successful at living this way. But we believe, with all our hearts that this is the right way to live, that it is the only way to true happiness, peace, and joy. May God help us relinquish our dependency on the things of this world and to place our trust in his provident care.

Prayer

Father, you have given us all the material things of the earth as gifts to nurture and share with others. Help us to be good stewards of the gifts we have received from you. Make us grateful, responsible, generous, and willing to give back to you with increase. Free us from all obsessions and help us to let go willingly so that others may share in the fruits of your bounty. Amen.

Questions for Reflection and Discussion

What does St. Paul mean when he says that the love of money is the root of all evil? Can you cite some contemporary examples of how the craving for material things has resulted in evil consequences?

How does the craving for money or material things affect our daily lives? How is it built into our culture?

What is stewardship? Why is it an appropriate and effective response to the problems of our culture's obsessions with money and materialism?

How does "letting go" of our dependence on money and material possessions free us to live simpler, happier lives?

Chapter Eight
Truth

Truth sets us free. Lies entangle us in a web of falsehood and make it impossible for us ever be really satisfied with our lives.

What is truth? The way things really are—not as we would want them to be. An honest assessment of the situation before us for better or worse. Integrity. Authenticity. No bull. Straight talk. As Jesus says, truth is simply saying "yes or no" instead of embellishing, making everything more complicated (cf. Mt. 5:37).

Why is truth so important? Human life can be seen as a lifelong struggle for understanding, for meaning. All our lives we search for the truth about ourselves and our world. Who am I? What am I supposed to do with my life? How do I find happiness, satisfaction, and meaning in my daily life? Who are we as a society or a culture? What are our basic values? How do we know that we are living right—as individuals and as a community?

Without truth, a sure standard for measurement, we are set adrift in life's quest. Worse, we may be deliberately misled. The massive propaganda machines developed by totalitarian states like Nazi Germany and the U.S.S.R daily feed people lies and, as a result, distort their understanding of life. The same can be said of media cultures that lead people to believe in fantasies of eternal youth or endless satisfaction of all our desires. Unless we are told the truth about ourselves and the world around us, we end up living in a land of make-believe unable to distinguish shadows from reality. This is the "brave new world" of science fiction—where people are inundated with pleasant lies to keep them docile, contented, and mildly productive like livestock in a corral or mental patients on drugs.

No matter how attractive they may seem, lies keep us in the dark. This is true whether they are "little white lies" or gravely serious untruths. If we lie to ourselves and deny the truth, we choose to stay in the shadows rather than be exposed to the full light of day. If we want to become mature human beings, we must be open to the truth about ourselves and our world no matter how painful it may seem. If we can't see clearly, we can't understand. And if we don't understand, we can't take whatever steps are necessary to change ourselves or our society to make life better, to make it real.

Jesus said, "I am the way, the truth, and the life." We believe that Jesus alone speaks the absolute truth about who we are, God's children, and what we are called to do with our lives: love God and love each other. Jesus' truth exposes the false promises we hear every day: New clothes will make you young again. Fast cars give us sex appeal. Youth and fame and fortune are the ultimate meaning of life. If you want to be happy, grab all the gusto you can.

We believe that Jesus' truth is countercultural, so naturally we don't want to hear it. It goes against the grain of our contemporary experience. Jesus shows us the advantages of living simply in a complex world. He urges us to surrender, to give up control and be spiritually poor, in a world that is obsessed with wealth and security. Jesus challenges us to see that accepting responsibility for others is not the unfair burden we're told it is, but in fact is the way to true freedom and happiness. Perhaps most important, Jesus' truth contradicts the totally false idea that our constant preoccupation with our own needs and wants can ever satisfy the longing in our heart of hearts.

Truth is a series of paradoxes: The one who surrenders will win. The last shall be first. To live we must first die to self. These are the truths that Jesus came to teach us. They are the truths he lived and died for. If we take them to heart and try to integrate them into our daily lives, we will have life abundantly. We will be joyous, happy, and free.

The teaching and example of Jesus show us the truth about ourselves and our world. Where else would we look to find the truth? Is there anyone else who "walks the talk" like Jesus? Media experts? Government officials? University professors? Pundits on the right or the left? Religious leaders? Is there anyone else who fully integrates into his or her daily life the principles that define what human life is all about? Is there anyone else who doesn't just speak the truth but who actually lives it—completely and perfectly—in his or her daily life?

There are many voices today that tell us "everything is relative" or "truth is just one person's opinion." We don't agree. We believe that there are, in fact, basic truths that we can count on in every time, place and circumstance.

We fully acknowledge that telling the truth (and living it) is not always easy—especially in a world that urges us to believe the convenient falsehoods that are all around us. Still, we believe that the truth is always worth searching for. We also believe that knowing and living the truth is essential to real freedom and lasting joy. We are called to be stewards of the truth—to guard and protect it and to share it generously with others in love.

Prayer

Lord Jesus Christ, you are the way, the truth, and the life. Help us to be open to the truth, to reject all forms of deception and falsehood, and to seek only what is real and good in our lives. Deliver us from the evils of selfishness and sin and lead us into the light of your truth—in our personal lives and in the political and social structures that govern human affairs. Lord, we believe that your truth will set us free. Help us to seek and find you—now and always and forever. Amen.

Questions for Reflection and Discussion

Why do Christians reject the popular ideas that "everything is relative" and that truth is "just one person's opinion"?

Why do we believe that Jesus not only speaks the truth but *is* the truth?

Why is telling the truth (and living it) so difficult?

What does it mean to be stewards of the truth? Can you give some examples of actions that constitute good stewardship of the truth?

CHAPTER NINE
LOVE

Human existence is a lifelong search for love. Our search begins in infancy and continues in different forms throughout every stage of life. There is never a time when we no longer need love—or when we stop searching for it one way or another.

We believe that it's important to understand, and channel appropriately, this powerful emotional, physical and spiritual desire, the quest for love. When it is expressed physically and emotionally, the quest for love takes the form of *eros*, which can be defined as sexual desire or romantic love. *Eros* has an important role to play in our lives—especially when we are seeking a lover, someone to share our life intimately and permanently as a husband or wife. *Eros* is a good thing, a source of romance, creativity, pleasure, and intimacy. But *eros* is not an end-in-itself, and if we confuse our erotic feelings and desires with the search for true and lasting love, we are bound to be bitterly disappointed, and ultimately dissatisfied, in our lifelong quest.

There is a lot of confusion in our contemporary culture about the relationship between *eros* and love. Advertising and the entertainment media tell us, often quite explicitly, that the way to satisfy our deep-seated desire for love is to stay young and attractive or to make ourselves more desirable to potential lovers. We are encouraged to want more erotic fulfillment, to seek excitement and pleasure wherever we can find it—all in the name of love. To help us gain fulfillment of our desires, our culture offers a seemingly endless supply of products and services that promise to make us younger, happier, more attractive, and more able to give and receive pleasure in our quest for romantic love. The result is usually disappointment, but instead of recognizing that our search for love can never be satisfied in this way, we too often move on to something else, the latest fad, hoping that this will bring us happiness where others have failed.

In fact, our culture urges us to be constantly restless and dissatisfied, especially in matters of romance and sexuality. We're led to believe that others (usually the rich and famous) have it better than we do—a more fulfilling life, better sex, opportunities to escape the boredom and frustration of everyday life. We are encouraged to want a more romantic lifestyle, to be envious of famous people who seem to have so much more than we do when it comes to love and romance.

The reality is quite different, of course. Those who appear to have it all rarely do, and as the stories of famous people often illustrate, they frequently are totally lost when it comes to satisfying their most fundamental emotional needs. As it turns out, the search for love is never successful when it's based on a covetous desire for what others have in the way of romance, sex appeal, or "the good life." If we really want to find love, it's best to look beyond the lifestyles of the rich and famous to the lives of the saints!

If most of our culture's pathways to love turn out to be dead ends, where should we go to find true love? The first eight chapters of this book describe what we believe is the source of love and its ultimate goal: God. We also discuss what we believe are the "places" where true love can be found: in the person of Jesus Christ, in the Church, in authentic family life, in respect for the dignity of human life, in authentic human sexuality, in the stewardship of all God's gifts, and in a commitment to understand (and live) the truth. We believe that God is love and that our lifelong quest is driven by a deep-seated spiritual hunger, our most profound desire, the search for God.

Where do we find this God who is love? How can we be sure we're looking in all the right places or that our motives are genuine?

Jesus said, "Blessed are the pure in heart, for they shall see God" (Mt. 5:8). To be pure of heart requires us to free ourselves of all selfish desires—to stop envying others and to be grateful for all that God has given them even when they appear to have more than we do. To be pure of heart requires that we be generous, willing to share everything we have with others, and that we be truly grateful for the ways that God has blessed us. If we are pure of heart, we will not spend all our time wishing we were different. We will be reasonably content and satisfied with who we are and what we have in life—knowing that, in the end, our hearts will never be fully satisfied until they find their final resting place in God.

The search for love is our lifelong mission or goal as human persons. This spiritual quest is completely different from our usual search for things that will satisfy our self-centered cravings. True love calls us outside of ourselves. It soothes our deepest longings and fulfills our basic loneliness by drawing our attention away from ourselves toward others. This is where true love can be found—not in the false or empty places that our erotic anti-culture proposes to us on a daily basis, but in a loving service to others based on gratitude, generosity and unselfishness.

Our lifelong search for love becomes a genuinely spiritual experience when it expresses itself in prayer (the desire to listen for God's will and to share our hopes and fears with him) and in charity (the desire to help others out of love for them and love for God).

As St. John says so beautifully, "God is love, and he who abides in love abides in God, and God abides in him" (1 Jn. 4:16b). We pray that the search for love will lead us to our hearts' desire, to a deeply spiritual experience, to Jesus the "joy of man's desiring," to the abiding love of God.

Prayer

God of love, you are the source and goal of everything that exists. You are the love we seek and the satisfaction that we long for every day of our lives. Help us to be pure of heart and to recognize you for the personal, loving God that you are. Help us to seek and find you in the unselfish and loving service we offer to others—especially those who are most in need. Loving God—Father, Son, and Holy Spirit—we know that our restless hearts will never be satisfied until they rest in you. Show us how to abide in you. Show us how to love. Amen.

✠

STEWARDS OF JOY: TAKING CARE OF AND SHARING THE GIFT OF FAITH

Questions for Reflection and Discussion

What's the difference between *eros* and love? How does our contemporary culture confuse these?

Where can we find true love? What does real love look like? How do we recognize it when we find it?

Why is the path to love that is promoted in the media and in advertising a dead end?

When is the search for love a genuinely spiritual experience?

CHAPTER TEN
JOY

If joy is the satisfaction of our deepest desires and longings as human beings, then true joy, ultimate joy, lasting joy, will only come with the fulfillment of our life's journey. Eternal joy is to be found in heaven, in the experience of God, and while this is a great mystery—something that we cannot even begin to describe adequately using the language of everyday experience—we are called to be stewards of this joyful hope, the promise of communion with God and all the saints in heaven.

To be a steward of joy means recognizing that God's greatest gift is yet to come. It means accepting that there is more to life than what we experience here and now. It also means taking on the responsibility to nurture the hope of heaven and to share it with others. A steward of joy is someone who refuses to settle for less than complete satisfaction. A steward of joy holds onto the promise that we will one day be united with God in what the poet W. B. Yeats calls "a world better far than this."

The most consistent temptation that most of us face in our daily lives is to settle for less. We seek happiness and fulfillment in the things of this world—in fame, fortune, or worldly success—or in material things like houses, cars, the latest fashions, or widescreen TVs. None of these things is bad. Everything that God made is good, but to search for the satisfaction of our heart's desire in worldly things can only lead to disappointment and, ultimately, to despair.

We believe that the purpose of human life is: "to know, love, and serve God, and to be happy with him in this life and in the next," as the Baltimore Catechism expressed it. As human beings, we are drawn beyond the satisfaction of our immediate needs and wants. Our most powerful inner drives are spiritual, and they urge us to look past life as we know it here on earth to eternal life with God. When we ignore our spiritual nature, or replace our quest for God with other things, we deny ourselves the chance to be truly happy. This is what hell is—the decision to cut ourselves off from what we long for most and to settle for something infinitely less satisfying.

With this in mind, we believe that the most serious, negative consequence of human sinfulness is the disorientation of our deepest desires. Sins of greed and envy, for example, arise from the confused notion that

57

more money or material things will make us truly happy, or from the really foolish idea that if we only had the possessions, power, and status that someone else has, our cravings for completeness would be satisfied.

A new house or car won't make us truly happy. More money in the bank is not the key to our success as human beings. Fame doesn't last. Power is an illusion. Youth and beauty always fade.

These things are not the meaning of life or the reason for our existence. At best, the material things that we desire are means to a worthwhile end: providing for life's necessities, raising a family and doing worthwhile work without having to worry constantly about where the money will come from to live a decent life.

We believe that it is important to recognize that we are constantly being tempted to settle for less than true and lasting joy. If we really want to be happy, we must resist these temptations and look beyond whatever is seducing us at the moment to a far more significant goal: being united with God and with everyone we love for all eternity in our heavenly home.

St. Augustine once described the hope of heaven this way: "God himself will be the goal of our desires; we shall contemplate him without end, love him without surfeit, praise him without weariness. This gift, this state, this act, like eternal life itself, will assuredly be common to all" (*Catechism of the Catholic Church* #2550).

We believe that we are called to nurture this great hope and to share it freely with everyone who seeks to discover the source and goal of their innermost longing, the desire for union with God. To carry out this profound responsibility, to share with others the hope-filled vision that is the promise of heaven, we must be people of real depth and integrity in our spiritual lives. We must be stewards of joy.

Prayer

Lord Jesus Christ, you are the meaning of the world and of human life. You are the goal of all our desires, the satisfaction of all our longings.

Help us to seek and find you. Teach us to reject the false promises and empty illusions of the world around us. May we open our hearts so that we can encounter you face-to-face in prayer, in the sacraments and in loving service to our sisters and brothers everywhere. Lord, by the power of your grace, fill our hearts with the joy that we seek so that we can be one with you now and in the world to come. Amen.

Questions for Reflection and Discussion

What does it mean to be stewards of joy—to nurture and share the hope of a better world to come?

How do selfishness and sin distort our deepest desires – causing us to seek fulfillment and satisfaction in all the wrong places?

How do we reorient our desires, our cravings, our most deeply spiritual longings? How do we find the right path to total satisfaction and fulfillment?

What does St. Augustine mean when he describes heaven in this way: "God himself will be the goal of our desires; we shall contemplate him without end, love him without surfeit, praise him without weariness."?

CONCLUSION
THE TEN COMMANDMENTS

The reader may have noticed that the ten chapters of this little book follow the basic structure of the Ten Commandments. Chapters 1-3 deal with God, the holy name of Jesus and the Church (which makes possible the Lord's Day). The remaining chapters deal with right-living—family life, respect for life, sexuality, money and material things, truthfulness, and rejecting "covetousness" in the search for love and joy. While this is not intended to be a commentary on the Ten Commandments, it became obvious during the preparation of this book that this would be an effective way to organize "what we believe" and to pass it on to others in a simple and straightforward way.

When the *Catechism of the Catholic Church* was being drafted, there was vigorous debate among the bishops who were responsible for the catechism's contents about whether it was appropriate to include the Ten Commandments. Some argued that negative, proscriptive laws were out of place in a compendium of Church teaching designed to "recover joy in the beauty of the faith and wonder over its vital energy." Others were concerned that the Decalogue's origins in the Old Testament, with its strong emphasis on the Law (Torah), would undermine the catechism's responsibility to call attention to New Testament themes of liberty and love.

In the end, the bishops decided in favor of including the Ten Commandments in the *Catechism of the Catholic Church*. As an integral part of the catechism's third section, "Life in Christ," the Ten Commandments find their rightful place in the context of a thorough discussion of themes of freedom, conscience, virtues, sin (personal and communal), and the Old and New Testaments' views of law and grace. Before exploring each of the Ten Commandments, the catechism makes it clear that each human person is called to holiness, which is understood to be "full collaboration between God's gracious help and human freedom." The old Law has been fulfilled in Christ, and it is possible now to live freely in conformity with the Law through cooperation with God's grace.

The *Catechism of the Catholic Church* does not gloss over the negative—even harsh—tone of the Ten Commandments. The sins that are prohibited in the Decalogue are serious. Unchecked, these deadly vices can cause profound injury, unhappiness, and death (spiritual and physical) to individuals and communities. These commandments are not meant to be mere "guidelines" or "helpful suggestions." They are absolutes. Without them, we are morally lost. Without them, we do not know how to live—as individuals or as communities.

At the same time, the *Catechism* teaches that the Ten Commandments can be seen as "laws of growth." Their faithful observance leads to the maturation of personality and to an increased sense of responsibility (stewardship) for the gifts we have been given by a good and loving God.

Today, we read about the Ten Commandments mainly in the context of arguments over public displays of religion in courthouses and other civic buildings. This is unfortunate. We believe the Ten Commandments are an amazing source of guidance and direction for daily living. Yes, they tell us *what not to do* if we want to be happy, holy people living in a state of grace. But the *Catechism's* loving exposition of the positive values reflected in each Commandment (cf. CCC 2084-2550) also offer wonderful insights into who we are as human persons created in God's image and how we are supposed to live as free people called to love God and one another.

TO ORDER ADDITIONAL COPIES OF THIS BOOK,
CONTACT:

Saint Catherine of Siena Press ...

...an Indianapolis-based publisher of inspirational and catechetical materials. You can learn more about this and other publications at:

www.saintcathpress.com
www.danconwayrsi.com
888-232-1492

OTHER STEWARDSHIP PUBLICATIONS AVAILABLE FROM SAINT CATHERINE OF SIENA PRESS:

Stewardship in America: A Countercultural Way of Life
Daniel Conway

What Do I Own and What Owns Me? A Spirituality of Stewardship
Daniel Conway

The Good Steward
Daniel Conway

I Like Being in Parish Ministry: Stewardship
Daniel Conway

More than Silver or Gold: Homilies of a Stewardship Priest
Daniel J. Mahan